Naps Are More Serious Than You Think

Naps Are More Serious Than You Think

Poems by

Cailin Iverson

• Auchentoroly Press •
Baltimore, Maryland

Copyright © 2014 by Cailin Iverson

All rights reserved. This book or any portion thereof may not be reproduced or used in any manner whatsoever without the express written permission of the publisher except for the use of brief quotations in a book review.

Printed in the United States of America

First Printing, 2014

ISBN 978-0-9960860-1-1

Auchentoroly Press
Baltimore, MD 00000

"The cat does not offer services. The cat offers itself."
–William S. Burroughs
The Cat Inside

For Nicole

Contents

Chocolate Covered Raisins   13
The Girl and the Snail   14
"chronic napping"   16
Lesson Learned   17
Gardening   18
My (Niece's) Bed   19
Just Like She Does   20
Snoozing   21
I've always wanted to ask   22
Army Brats on Veterans Day   24
I'll Just Stay Here   25
Where Do I Go From Here?   26
Heritage in Cigarette   27
"Would you like anything to drink, miss?"   28
No One is Off Limits   29
Fort Dix   30
Just Another Day at Work   32
Head Rush   33
When I wake in the morning   34
Hello Again   35
What Stage of Grief is This?   36
Dinner for One   38
There must be something to learn   39
Moving Furniture   40
Accommodating Loneliness   41

Chocolate Covered Raisins

My mother kept a stash of chocolate covered raisins
in the door of the fridge that were only for her,
but during a Minnesotan summer night,
my sister and I hunted fireflies, mosquitos
attacked our legs, the sun stalked the horizon,
and when the hunt was over
we ran in the house, wiped the sweat
from our upper lips and along our hairline,
catching our breath. By then, I couldn't resist
the forbidden treat, a smooth, cool melt that tickled
my tongue and trickled down my throat,
the raisin another sweet surprise.

It wasn't until headlights beamed
through the kitchen windows
that I grew nervous, and subtle panic
set in, my sister wearing a smirk.
Mom noticed the child's handful missing
with her keen eyes, but I didn't confess,
and let my sister go down with me.
We were grounded for a week and immediately
sent to bed. I fell asleep that night
to the cries of my sister asking why
I didn't tell the truth and to the clinking ice
in Mom's drink.

The Girl and the Snail

I was wearing a pink ruffle bikini
on the edge of my grandfather's dock.
He's been dead nearly ten years
but he's there on his porch,
a whiskey in hand and prosthetic leg
propped on a seventies green flowered
lawn chair, smiling (he never smiled) and assuring
(he never assured either) my nervous steps
to the edge. I lay on my baby-fat belly, reach
in the cool green water and feel
the snails clinging to the dock frame.

I pluck one from a cluster
and at eye-level, it whispers
"just let it go," and winks an antenna eye
and smiles with a mouth that's not really there
as I drop him back in the water
with quiet ripples and I watch
him sink, his smile still beaming
and his eye still winking,
the other staring at me
the whole way down
to a murky sand cloud his little body made
at the bottom.

I look back at my grandfather
who waves goodbye
and turns back to his house.

I stand

and I jump.

"chronic napping"

Google:
Chronic Fatigue Syndrome Forum: Naps: Medical Questions
chronicnapping.blogspot.com: 1 post: March 2012:
Not about napping
How to Nap (Without Feeling Exhausted Afterwards)

Facebook:
Chronic Napping: Interest: Four likes

Twitter:
I can literally nap away any problem ever
except for my chronic napping problem. @duhmynameisstacy
Health Issues: No-nonsense Napping Guide for Toddlers:
Experts explain. @NJPain
Chronic napping is not Gucci. @gospeldancemusiclover

Tumblr:
I need a nap...and by nap I mean small coma
so I can hide from my life.
Dear Naps, I'm sorry I was mean to you in kindergarten.
A picture of a sleeping kitten inside an Ugg boot.

Lesson Learned

My baby doll had blue eyes that closed when laid down,
with tan plastic arms and feet, a plush body. I kept her
in a blue dress with white flower embroidery. We'd climb
the sappiest of trees, ones with prickles and pine needles,
branches thick and step worthy. They'd taper off the farther up,
thinning and thinning to its top reach– the unattainable goal
for this five, six, or eight-year-old girl. I'd have my baby doll
in one hand and a blanket in the other for an imaginary picnic
in the jungle canopy of Fort Dix, saddling a mid-level branch
serving tea and raspberry danish. Until one day we came home
covered in sap after being told to keep our feet on the ground.
Her dress was torn. My feet like tape. The blanket stained.
We were grounded for three days, forced to separate rooms;
our extremities scrubbed almost raw. And when I saw her again,
reunited, we grabbed the same blanket, put on a pair of shoes,
and chose a less sappy tree.

Gardening

I understood germination at five
as I nursed a marigold seed
in a paper cup. Grandpa dampened
the paper towel ground. We watched the sprout
poke through, twist as it grew, climbing
the white plastic walls while he sipped
morning coffee and deciphered
loon calls from the lake out front.

After breakfast, I'd watch him water
his garden of rhubarb with an eighty-year
ease, a green thumb we Brostroms have
that I may have missed. Because the marigolds
never actually bloomed, birthday bouquets
never lasted, and I killed dad's lemongrass
last summer.

My (Niece's) Bed

I napped in the bottom bunk
that my nieces now use
when sleeping over at Mom's,
its walls dark red, a change my sister made
when she moved back home, quite different
from my baby blue and farm animal border
I picked at when mad or bored.

The glow-in-the-dark stars
still stuck on the popcorn ceiling now dim and dirty,
dust clinging to corners and light bulbs.

My nieces chose fleece sheets of purple, pink,
and blue polka dots, the same colors as my polka dotted
clay fish that hung from a planter's hook.
My seashell light switch was also replaced,
the carpet now off-white instead of sixties blue,
and the bed is against the wrong wall. But even though

I haven't slept in that bed or room in fifteen years,
I woke from that nap dazed
by its deepness, the sun shining
through a crack
in sheer black curtains.

Just Like She Does

I got this illness
this debilitating habit insurance would deem
pre-existing or maybe even
genetic,

where I get in this mood
with vodka-crans and whiskey gingers.

Where I strip down to bra and panties,
sing and dance to Zeppelin while one cat

hides in fear and the other
chases my heels.

I drink all night, like my mother with gin
and Prince, her prancing the basement.

But when I look in my full-length mirror
at the way my eyes glass over, I see
her slanted smile, her lazy eyelids.

I sleep the whole next day and wake
craving salt to mask my acid tongue, just
like she does.

Snoozing

I was once fired for sleeping at my desk
like I did in grade school, leaving wrinkle marks
across my face.
And I don't mean these easy
twenty-minute power naps
old men take in their La-Z-Boys or office couches,
but multi-hour, five stage R.E.M journeys,
until a cat gathers a few of my curls in his mouth
and yanks, an alarm for his evening dinner,.
Though I simply snooze
and pull the sheet
over my head.

I've always wanted to ask

      when was the last time
      someone took you out
      with the intention of seeing
      your modest queen-sized four post
      draped in gray curtains,
      black and white pet hair, a plum
      duvet, your favorite Icart
      on the wall.

      Or if there was a woman you've met
      while walking Michon and Filou,
      she walking another Havanese.
      You'd talk of rescues, volunteering, or historical
      societies you each belong to. You'd take her back
      to your 1830s stucco, let her smell your antique perfume,
      and let her
      make morning mimosas
      on the wrap-around porch.

      So one time over dinner, I asked why
      you never married, why
      I've never seen
      another's hand in yours
      or heard whispers
      of Manhattan love affairs, and you replied:

"two men asked in college,
and I declined them both."
Then you tapped
your fire engine nails
against your martini glass,
downing the rest as an end
to conversation, and we went out
for ice cream on Grand
while I pondered your use of *and*
instead of *but*.

Army Brats on Veteran's Day

I've never thanked my dad
for his twenty-year service, or saving
my baby passport, my grandfather's
Naval map, Nicole's folded flag.
I've never thanked him for feeling safe
behind barbed wire fences
and never locking our doors;
MPs always patrolling, always
standing guard.

One time off base, when my purse was stolen
off my shoulder, and my hips dragged
against pavement, he showed up tipsy and unafraid,
ready to get me a carry and conceal,
training I never received.

Veteran's Day is almost over
but I still won't call, won't thank him
for being around today
when he wasn't so often
before, won't thank him
for telling me war, life, and human
stories, won't thank him
for telling me
to tell my own.

I'll Just Stay Here

Every day I succumb to the soft cold
of my turned over pillow as I fight
the incessant pawing at my shoulders,
the sandpaper licks
at the corner of my eyes, and the nose
in my nose, trying to breathe
the life, the hunger of a cat
into me. It's a morning routine
that rarely happens in the morning
but afternoon, like a teenager
full of time.

Where Do I Go From Here?

There are strings of silk
running from bush to rock
to cigarette butt, strings or wide webs,
maybe a connection or path
seemingly random, as if wasted,
not intoxicated but dwindled,
not beaten or pushed, but low
on fuel. Though producing, changing,
there's a lack of growth and direction.

Heritage in Cigarettes

My first cigarette on a foggy morning
always reminds me of where I come from.
Not as in which state or military base,
but heritage.
I feel it when the smoke lingers
and clogs deep pores
in and around my Norse nose,
a weight I wipe with the back of my hand,
much like I imagine my ancestors did
with their dirt-known hands,
who also slaughtered their meals,
harvested vegetable greens, yellows, and reds,
ripped when ripe or gold and sold for just enough
to roll a few more cigarettes
and brace for the coming winter.

"Would you like anything to drink, miss?"

>Not even twenty-four hours have passed
>since I promised, or maybe just said,
>that I wouldn't drink for a while. Not
>dry-uary or two-week detox, just
>"a while;" and actually, it's been fifteen
>hours, but a flight upgrade to first-class
>means complimentary and immediate
>service. Maybe I should have told the ticket agent
>no thank you, or opted for an exit row,
>but whatever, I ordered a ginger ale instead
>and kept that promise
>for three whole days.

No One is Off Limits

For twenty-six years and counting,
I have loved men. Specifically, ones with glasses
I'll eventually break. Ones with five months
of Scottish stubble and a jaw I often touch
or slap. Most are taller than my five-seven frame,
thicker than my thin Irish bones, their bellies bigger
than my Midwestern pouch, so I don't feel
insecure. Though last summer, I fell in love
with a girl. Specifically, one with perfect 20/20,
her gaze electric and her face of Georgian peaches,
skin pale and unblemished. She was shorter at five-four
with thicker, Danish bones I'd tickle, her belly
not bigger, but East Coastal thick.
I'd trace it with ease before we settled down,
deep down. And now I know that no one
is off limits.

Fort Dix

I can't even say I've lived in Jersey
because I never left base.

I attended Fort Dix Elementary School.
We shopped at the commissary
and PX, got gas and Snickers at the
Shoppette, and hung out in a four-block radius
around the house.

It was an ordinary base filled with gunners,
children, and busy-bored Army wives,
but I only remember every detail of Cedar Street,
the rest like photographs.

A red poppy field not meant to be walked through,
so I ran.

Trees, trees and trees
grown to be climbed,
kids hanging like Christmas
ornaments.

The look on my face
when I realized I lived
in an armored location.

The surrounding fence
with barbed wire
at the top.

Just Another Day at Work

June 24th, 2008, Sadr City, Iraq

You probably showered, lathered yourself
in cucumber bubbles, your hair in rosemary,
and dried off with pima cotton towels.

You probably applied your make-up, a lipstick
I called burnt red, maybe a pump or two
of Bvlgari on your neck and inside wrists.

You probably thought you were going
to just another meeting, another sheik,
another dispute to mediate, but you didn't know
there were explosives in the walls.

You didn't see the insurgents start to run.
You didn't hear the blast
off dirt streets. You didn't smell
the melting skin. You didn't feel
your heart stop beating. And you didn't taste

the saline, the grief
rolling off my cheeks
when the generals climbed our steps,
sat at our table, and told me
you were gone.

Head Rush

My sister and I reminisce
about how we no longer chase
the head rush of handstands and cartwheels,
the heavy heartbeat of running home
in a thunderstorm with eyes directed
at the green-hued sky and smiles as wide
as our cheeks could stand, the speed
we'd roller blade down forest trails,
and the shock of skinny dipping
off the banks of the Mississippi;
how our mouths have tightened
with life around bottles of Old English
and hand-blown glass pipes.

When I wake in the morning

it's not an internal clock
but a cat's chilly paw
against my cheek, padded feet that
prance on my bed, back, and arms.
Wet noses give eskimo kisses
as if checking for breath,
but no, I am very much alive
though not willing to stir
after patchy sleep and subdued sunrise,
because even trees fold their branches
when snow weighs heavy
and they cling to their roots
when wind howls; I feel it
through brick wall cracks
and Nyxi's fur as she nuzzles my hand,
I hear it through single-pane windows
and Zak's throat crying with hunger.

I may not get out of bed
at all today,
I don't want my feet
as cold as theirs.
I don't want my voice
to strain like theirs.
I just want to sink down
and let the bed
be my earth.

Hello, Again

Last night I slept in a bed
I haven't slept in for six months, but his memory
foam accepted my body just the same, cushioning
my jutted hips, the top curves of my feet, the support
we stomach-sleepers need. I didn't even feel
him move, his shifts, twists, and turns, the rearrangement
of not two, not three, but four pillows. The down comforter
he wrapped us in, entwined our legs, placing his hand
under my cheek as I kissed his wrist.
But I scooted out and away as soon as I heard
the light, soft snores of his sleep. I needed cooler temperatures,
right to the cusp of goosebumps.

What Stage of Grief is This?

It's been almost a year since last I
saw you. Your name and number still
programmed in my cell, your email
still in my address book, but I can't remember

your call, our conversation. And since
you always avoided the camera, I only have
one picture of you on a couch, smiling to
someone else out of frame.

A few days after the funeral I went
home to your closet and remembered helping Dad
pick out your final outfit, asking things like:
Does she need a bra or underwear?
Does she need shoes?
What would she want to wear?

I felt like I should have known the
answers, or there was a norm to adhere to
but I didn't know, and didn't research, settling
for a classic black skirt, blazer, and lavender cami.

And when it was deemed time
to sort through your clothes, I never got very far,
always crying among a pile of clothes
that still smelled like your Bvlgari perfume,

the scent so overpowering, but I couldn't
find the bottle.

You probably had it with you, now
lost among desert sand
and a crumbled city.

Dinner, Alone

I'm treating myself to a twenty-four dollar dinner
at a place called The Bookstore, a converted library
with built-in shelves, wooden globes, a bust of Galileo,
and where water is served in Jim Bean bottles.
When given the drink list I brush the waitress off,
but she replies: you could be better with whiskey.
I chuckle politely because unknown to her, I'm still hung-over
with a dripping, burning nose from the Paxil I crushed
and snorted out of boredom,
my eyes still poufy from crying on the shoulder of a friend
who voiced concern, from crying all day between dozes
in a city hotel room and Words with Friends.
And now as I sit with these posh patrons
sipping their double-malts taking candle-lit selfies,
I fight the urge to order a glass of Malbec
to go with my medium-rare steak and sautéed
organic vegetables, as if one glass
is all I would have.

There must be something to learn

as I dry heave, spit, and involuntarily cry
into a toilet bowl that's shared
between strangers, my face in awe
as my body tries to retch
these things from my stomach
that'll be gone by tomorrow
but I'll always see the judgment
in strangers' eyes.

Moving Furniture

Dad has a drawer full of memories,
the second from the top of a mass-produced dresser
of fake wood with dents and bruises
bearing its grain and age.
This drawer used to house Nicole's socks
and now the flag that draped her coffin,
the ash boxes of her dogs, Sylvie and Solze, their names
etched in gold plates. They rest on top of pictures
she took of Dad, my sister, and I on the couch,
a random afternoon spent in pjs watching CNN.

It's been years but we handle this drawer, our past,
like moving furniture, removing, replacing,
not pausing besides a shuffle through photographs,
like how I imagine lives flash
before dying.

Accommodating Loneliness

My bed is forming a permanent groove down the middle,
I haven't really left it in a week. I even moved the cat's litter box
to the foot of my attic stairs, the smell of shit and piss
clumped in corn meal, the World's Best Cat Litter.

It's nauseating, suffocating even,
but my resolve to stay in bed is stronger
so I accommodate this loneliness, this defense,
and only wake to nibble
on saltines and dry cheerios
while softly crying.

Acknowledgements

I'd like to thank Team Auchentoroly, whose members include Gabe Luzier, Drew Robison, and Jamie McLane, my three superheros. My thesis group, UB's Creative Writing & Design faculty, and fellow classmates, who have all helped shape my craft, this book, and my overall being, for which I am eternally grateful. I'd also like to tip my hat to an outsider, but great friend, Kendall Bailey, for his brilliant and bountiful aide. The rest goes to my familial, friendship, four-legged, and future loves: this is (me) for you.